Dan the Dancer

Lisa Weir
Photography by Siân Bradfield

Contents

Dance

This is Dan.
Dan likes to dance.

There are all kinds of dances.
Let's find out about some of them.

A Battle Dance

The **Haka** is a kind of dance.
It was danced before battles.
Now it is danced to welcome visitors and at sports games.

This dance is from New Zealand.

Look at Dan!

Dan bends his knees.
He lifts his arm.

A Jumping Dance

The jumping dance is a kind of dance. Dancers see how high they can jump.

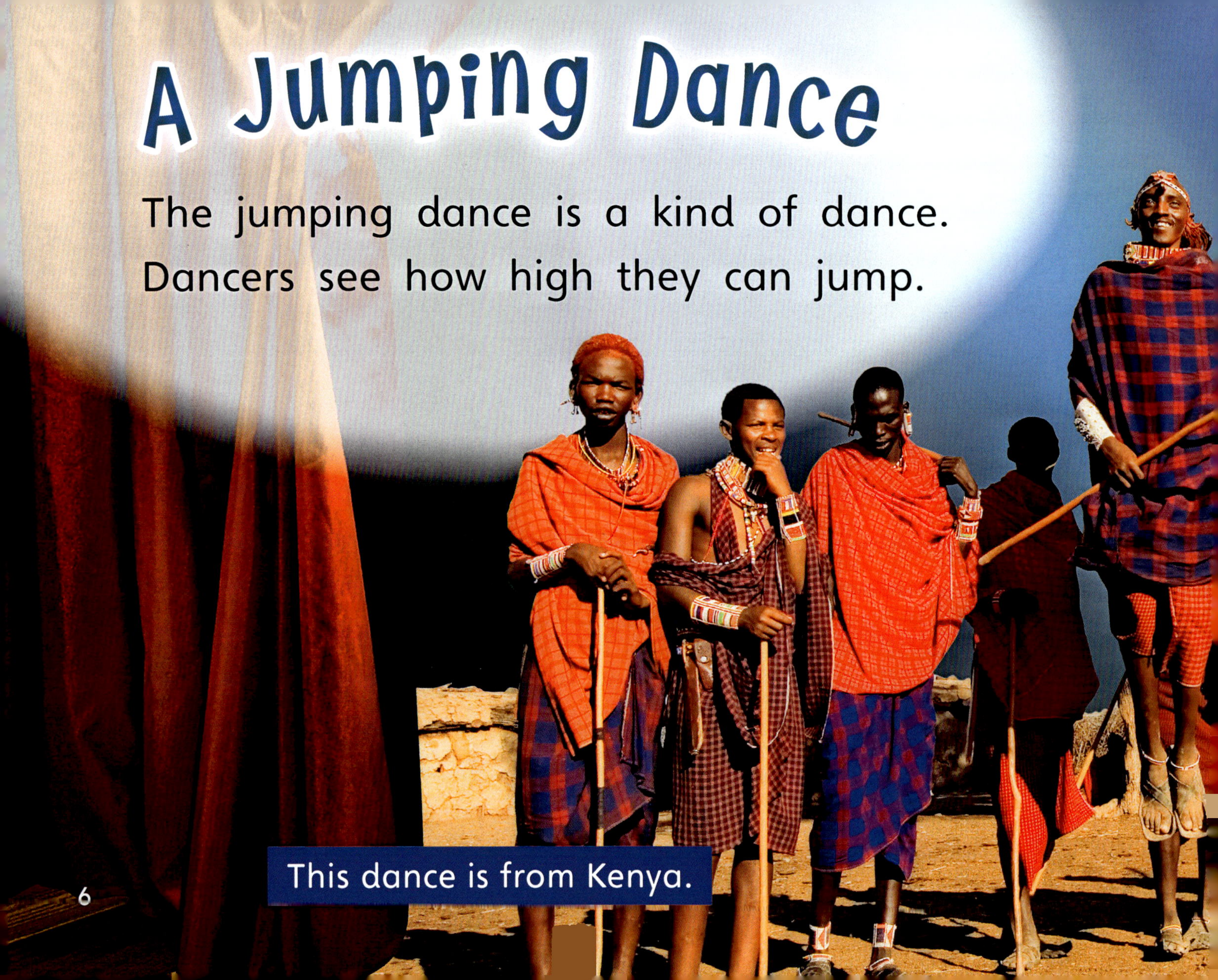

This dance is from Kenya.

Look at Dan!

Dan jumps high in the air.
His heels do not touch
the ground.

A Bollywood Dance

Bollywood dancing is a kind of dance. It is made up of old dances and new dances. The dancers wear **costumes**.

This dance is from India.

Look at Dan!

Dan twists his body.
He hops from foot to foot.

A Ballet Dance

Ballet is a kind of dance.

Ballet dancers have many steps to learn.

They can dance on their toes.

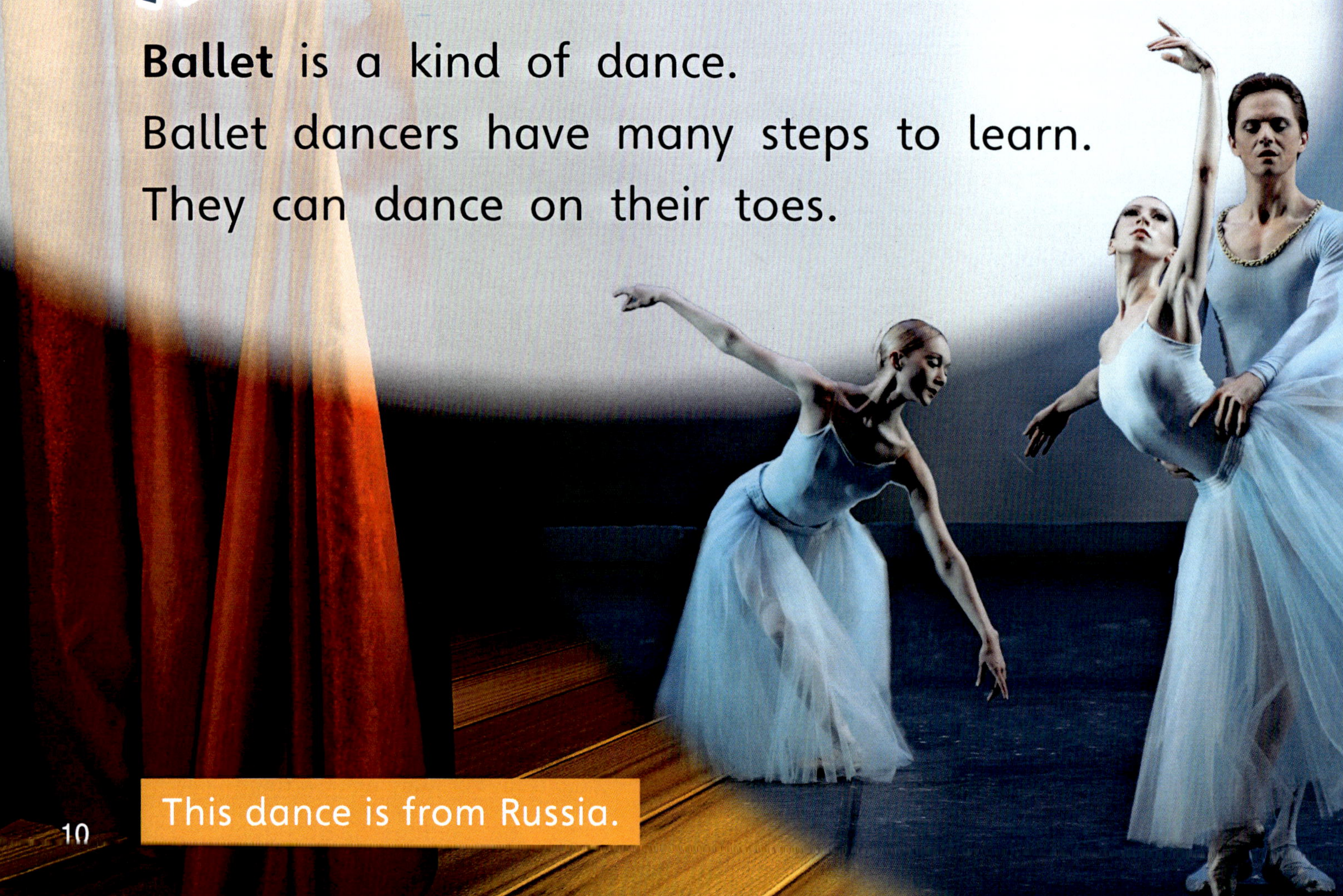

This dance is from Russia.

Look at Dan!

Dan jumps high into the air.
His legs are straight.

A Stepping Dance

Irish dancing is a kind of dance. Dancers jump, hop and side step. They keep their arms and hands by their sides!

This dance is from Ireland.

Look at Dan!

Dan moves his feet.
He keeps his arms by his side.

Dancing Is Fun

Dan likes dancing.

It is fun!

Look at Dan!

Dan likes to play soccer, too. He moves his feet and jumps, just like when he is dancing!

Glossary

ballet	a formal style of dance that usually tells a story
Bollywood	a type of film made in India
costumes	clothes worn for a particular activity
Haka	traditional dance of the Maori people in New Zealand
Irish dancing	traditional dancing from Ireland